WARSHIP PICTORIAL # 20

H. M. S. HOOD

by Steve Wiper

Computer Graphics by Thomas Schmid

CLASSIC WARSHIPS PUBLISHING

P. O. Box 57591 • Tucson, AZ. 85732 • USA

Web Site: www.classicwarships.com • Ph/Fx (520)748-2992

ISBN # 0-9745687-1-6

Printed by Arizona Lithographers, Tucson, Arizona

HISTORY OF THE BATTLECRUISER HOOD

November 1915: Royal Navy Admiralty request the construction of four very large battlecruisers armed with 15in. guns and speeds of 33 knots.

21 April 1916: Admiralty Board placed orders for three battlecruisers; *Hood* (John Brown Shipyard), *Howe* (Cammell Laird Shipyard) and *Rodney* (Fairfield Shipyard). The fourth, *Anson* (Armstrong Shipyard) was placed later.

1 September 1916: *Hood's* keel was laid at John Brown & Company Ltd., shipyards in Clydebank, Glasgow, Scotland, as ship #460.

13 September 1916: Improvements began on this day to original design were made to deck and turret protection of the approved design. This was because of the problems encountered with the RN battlecruisers at the Battle of Jutland back in May.

9 March 1917: The Admiralty suspended construction of *Howe*, *Rodney* and *Anson*.

22 August 1918: *Hood* was christened by Lady Hood, widow of Sir Horace Hood, lost at Jutland.

October 1918: Admiralty cancels rest of this class of battlecruisers.

7 August 1919: First main gun installed.

9 January 1920: *Hood* departs Clydebank to conduct builders and steam trials.

12-13 January 1920: En route to Rosyth.

19 January 1920: At Rosyth for post trials drydocking.

Late February 1920: Departed Rosyth and returned to Clydebank.

8 March 1920: Official trials commenced.

23-24 March 1920: En route to Rosyth.

April 1920: Post trials refit at Rosyth. Fore topgallant mast removed. A 15ft. rangefinder fitted on the control top. Aircraft platforms fitted atop both B and Y turrets.

15 May 1920: At Rosyth. *HMS Hood* was commissioned with 967 crewmen transferred from *HMS Lion*.

18 May 1920: *Hood* became Flagship, Battle Cruiser Squadron, Atlantic Fleet. Departed for Plymouth.

29 May-1 July 1920: "Spring Cruise" to Scandinavia. Ships of the Battle Cruiser Squadron, *Hood*, *HMS Tiger* (battlecruiser) and eight accompanying destroyers, visit various Scandinavian lands and also a show of force to dissuade Bolshevik actions in the Baltic states.

Winter 1920: Refit at Plymouth. Compass platform raised 5ft. and old windows blocked off. New roof and windows fitted, plus other minor modifications made to the bridge. After concentrating position added to after superstructure.

17 January-18 March 1921: Spring cruise in Spanish waters.

30 March-21 May 1921: At Rosyth. Drydocked for hull cleaning, refit and repairs.

June-July 1921: At Devonport for a refit. 8ft. rangefinder fitted to bridge and boat davits fitted P & S abreast mainmast.

13-15 July 1921: Exercises with Atlantic Fleet.

Autumn 1921: At Rosyth for a refit. Bridge enclosed. Two searchlights removed from towers between the funnels. Carley floats and a cutter fitted. Torpedo rangefinder fitted to foremast searchlight platform. Shelter deck cut back above 5.5in secondary weapons to allow full elevation.

17 January-8 April 1922: Spring Cruise to Spain and Mediterranean with *HMS Tiger*, *Repulse* and *Renown* (battlecruisers). Visited Gibraltar, Malga, Valencia, Vigo and Toulon. Also operated temporarily with *HMS Warspite* and *Valiant* (battleships).

17 April-8 May 1922: At Rosyth. *Hood* was drydocked for cleaning, repairing and painting of the ship.

5 July 1922: At Torbay. King George V aboard to inspect ship's company.

7-8 July 1922: En route to Devonport. While en route, conducted firing practice against former *SMS Nürnberg*, now a target ship.

20 August-2 November 1922: Brazilian and West Indies cruise with *Repulse*. At Rio de Janeiro, purpose of visit was to represent Great Britain during Brazilian Independence celebration. Members of *Hood's* crew participated in a "mini Olympics" against members of other navies, including Argentina, Brazil, Mexico, and the United States.

10 January-31March 1923: Spring cruise to Spain and Mediterranean with Atlantic Fleet.

14 May-21 June 1923: At Devonport for modernization.

26 June-18 July 1923: Scandinavian cruise as flagship of Battle Cruiser Squadron with *Repulse*.

27 July-3 September 1923: At Devonport for a refit and drydocking. Wireless radio installed on after control platform. Main topgallant mast fitted. Two 36in. searchlights fitted between the funnels.

16-31 October: At Rosyth. Drydocked for minor repairs.

27 November-29 September 1924: "Empire Cruise" or "World Cruise". *Hood* and *Repulse* participated in this famous public relations cruise around the world. The two battlecruisers were accompanied by the First Light Cruiser Squadron, steaming almost 40,000 knotical miles. They visited many ports in both the Atlantic and Pacific Oceans on this ten month journey.

28 September-5 November 1924: Devonport for partial refit. Main topgallant mast replaced with flagpole. 9ft. rangefinders replaced with 12ft. on foretop. Two 36in. searchlights between funnels removed.

7-23 November 1924: At Rosyth for drydocking.

25 November–14 January 1925: Devonport for drydocking to complete refit. Two searchlights between funnels removed.

19 January-29 March 1925: Spring cruise to Portugal, Spain and Mediterranean.

1 April-8 May 1925: At Devonport for refit and additional alterations.

15 July 1925: Participated in Battle Cruiser Squadron Regatta.

28 July-1 September 1925: At Devonport for repairs.

20 October-21 November 1925: Rosyth for drydocking.

23 November-12 January 1926: At Devonport for refit. Searchlights repositioned on after control platform. 15ft. high angle director fitted in front of searchlights. After control platform expanded. Gasoline lockers for ships boats fitted to shelter deck. Gaff added to mainmast.

12 January-27 March 1926: Spring cruise to Spain and Mediterranean.

29 March-3 May 1926: At Devonport for alterations.

31 May-4 June 1926: Trials off the Isle of Arran.

15 July-2 September 1926: Portsmouth for drydocking.

30 October 1926: Participates in tactical exercises with the Atlantic Fleet off Portland.

17 November-17 January 1927: At Devonport for refit. Signal searchlight moved for Admirals bridge to control tower platform. Torpedo rangefinder on foremost platform removed. Concentration dials removed. 9ft. rangefinder fitted on roof of compass platform.

17 January-26 March 1927: Spring cruise to Spain and Mediterranean.

28 March-2 May 1927: At Devonport for repairs.

8 July-30 August 1927: At Portsmouth for drydocking.

7 November-4 January 1928: At Devonport for a refit.

10 January-22 March 1928: Spring cruise to Spain and Mediterranean.

3 April 1928: Participates in tactical exercises with the Atlantic Fleet off Portland.

4-30 April 1928: At Devonport for repairs and refit.

27 June-2 August 1928: At Portsmouth for refit.
3 August-5 September 1928: Moved to Devonport to finish refit.
15 November-9 January 1929: At Devonport for repairs.
10 January-7 April 1929: Spring cruise to Spain and Mediterranean.
6 April 1929: Flagship of Battle Cruiser Squadron transferred to *Repulse*.
7 April-1 May 1930: At Devonport for minor repairs.
17 May 1929-16 June 1931: At Portsmouth, *Hood* was paid off and put in for a major two year refit and modernization. A catapult and aircraft handling crane were fitted on quarterdeck, aft of Y turret. Compass platform enlarged. Range clocks removed. Torpedo lookout platform extended. Lookout positions fitted on the control top. Two eight barreled 2pdr. Pom-Pom (40mm) AA mounts fitted P & S on the shelter deck between the funnels. Aircraft platform removed from atop the X turret. Carley floats added. Fuel bunkerage increased by 720 tons, using double bottom.
26 June 1931: Loses Fairey 3F floatplane on take off at Weymouth.
11 July 1931: Flag of the Battle Cruiser Squadron, Atlantic Fleet, transferred from *Renown*.
21 July-8 September 1931: At Portsmouth for overhaul. While there, participated in Portsmouth Navy Week.
11-16 September 1931: At Invergordon. Some members of *Hood's* crew involved in "Invergordon Mutiny" over a proposed reduction in pay rates for Royal Navy sailors.
19 November-6 January 1932: Portsmouth for repairs.
6 January-7 March 1932: Spring cruise to West Indies and Caribbean with *HMS Repulse*, *Norfolk*, *Dorsetshire* (heavy cruisers) and *Delhi* (light cruiser).
13 March-14 May 1932: At Portsmouth for repairs.
14-15 July 1932: Fleet exercises.
21 July-30 August 1932: At Portsmouth for repairs and a refit. Both of the 9ft. rangefinders removed from the control top. Catapult and aircraft crane removed from the quarterdeck. Participated in Portsmouth Navy Week.
30 August 1932: Recommissioned as Flagship, Battle Cruiser Squadron, Home Fleet
17 November-9 January 1933: Portsmouth for repairs.
11 January–25 March 1933: Spring cruise to Spain and Mediterranean. Based in Gibraltar.
16 June-6 September 1933: At Portsmouth for refit and modernization. Two 0.50cal. quad AA mounts and two 9ft. rangefinders fitted P & S on the signal platform. Aircraft platform removed from atop B turret.
10-26 September 1933: Flagship duties temporarily transferred to *Renown*.
24-26 October 1933: Exercises with Fleet.
13 November-6 January 1934: Portsmouth for repairs.
12 January–23 March 1934: Spring cruise to Spain and Mediterranean. Based at Gibraltar. Participated in Combined Fleet spring exercises.
27 March-11 May 1934: At Portsmouth for drydocking and repairs.
24 July-7 September 1934: At Portsmouth for repairs and painting. While there, participated in Navy Week.
14 November-14 January 1935: At Portsmouth for drydocking and repairs.
15-24 January 1935: Spring cruise to Spain and Mediterranean. En route to Gibraltar, collided with *Renown*. *Hood* sustained minor damage to hull and starboard propellers.
25-30 January 1935: At Gibraltar. Minor repairs accomplished. Departed Gibraltar for Portsmouth.
30 January-22 February 1935: Flag of Battle Cruiser Squadron temporarily transferred to *Repulse*.
4 February-5 March 1935: At Portsmouth for repairs to collision damage in drydock.
5-21 March 1935: Return to Gibraltar for Spring cruise and exercises.
25 March-13 May 1935: At Portsmouth for repair of defects from last refit.
16 July 1935: Participated in the Silver Jubilee Review for King George V off Spithead.
17 July-30 August 1935: *Hood* at Portsmouth to finish repairs and participated in Portsmouth Navy Week.
31 August 1935: On exercises.
Late 1935-13 January 1936: At Gibraltar.
16 January-21 February 1936: At Portsmouth for drydocking for minor hull repairs.
22 February-20 June 1936: Spring cruise to Spain and Mediterranean. Based at Gibraltar.
19 June 1936: Repairs to damaged turbine made at Gibraltar due to congestion at Portsmouth Dockyard.
23 June-10 October 1936: At Portsmouth to finish turbine repairs and cleaning of steam condensers. While there, *Hood* was refitted. 36in. searchlight platform was removed from foremast, compass platform expanded and an 8ft. rangefinder fitted. Forebridge expanded, after control platform expanded and additional platforms fitted on the mainmast.
22 July 1936: Battle Cruiser Squadron moves to Mediterranean Fleet administration
August 1936: Participates in Portsmouth Navy Week.
12 September-30 November 1936: Flag temporarily transferred to *HMS Barham* (battleship).
10 October 1936: Departed for Gibraltar, based there with Mediterranean Fleet.
January 1937: Based at Gibraltar and also exercised off Malta and Greece.
3-27 February 1937: At Malta for drydocking.
March 1937: On exercises. Based at Gibraltar.
23 March-3 April 1937: At Malta for changing of damaged propellers.
April 1937: On patrol in Bay of Biscay.
23 April 1937: The steamers *SS MacGregor*, *Hamsterly* and *Stanbrook* were carrying food and supplies from France to Spain when they were confronted by Nationalist warships. *Hood* was on patrol near the point at which they would enter the Spanish war zone. The convoy radioed for help. Nationalist warships fired across one merchant vessel's bows and directly challenged British destroyers in escort. *Hood* had to become involved and forced the Nationalist warships to stand down. The three cargo vessels ultimately made it safely to Spain.
7 May 1937: At Spithead for the Coronation Review of His Majesty King George VI.
20 May 1937: *Hood* visited by King George VI for inspection of flagship.
19 June-24 August 1937: Based at Malta and participated in the Autumn Cruise of Mediterranean Fleet.
26 July-20 August 1937: Repairs at Malta.
10-30 September 1937: At Malta for drydocking and minor hull repairs.
October 1937: Operating in Spanish waters on Neutrality Patrols.
6 November-5 January 1938: At Malta for drydocking. While there, *Hood* underwent a refit. Two 0.50cal. quad AA mounts fitted P & S on the after control platform. One eight barreled 2pdr. Pom-Pom fitted on shelter deck ahead of the after control platform.
January 1938: Operating in Spanish waters.
5 February-3 March 1938: At Malta in preparation for Combined Fleet spring exercises. Drydocked.
March-April 1938: Operating in Spanish waters on Neutrality Patrol.
7 May-28 June 1938: *Hood* at Malta in preparation for the Summer Cruise of the Mediterranean Fleet. Drydocked.
July 1938: Operated in waters off Greece and Spain.
9 August 1938: While en route to France, rescued crew of steamer *SS Lake Lugano*, which had been bombed by

Nationalist aircraft.
August 1938: Operated in Spanish waters with *HMS Sussex* (heavy cruiser).
20 September 1938: Grounded while leaving Gibraltar harbor, sustained minor damage.
28 September-1 October 1938: Departed Gibraltar, with 3rd Destroyer Flotilla, escorted troopship *SS Aquitania*.
October 1938: Operated in Spanish and French waters in the Mediterranean.
3 November 1938: En route for Marseille with 150 Spanish refugees aboard.
9 November-10 January 1939: At Malta for drydocking and repairs to Y turret.
9 January 1939: Flag transferred to *Barham*, as *Hood* departed for England.
18 January-13 August 1939: At Portsmouth for a major refit. Four 4in single AA mounts replaced with twin shielded mounts on the shelter deck between the aft funnel and the mainmast P & S. Director for the 2pdr. AA mounts fitted atop the after control platform. Two high angle directors fitted on the signal platform P & S. Four 40in. searchlights fitted on platforms P & S located on the after signal platform and the aft funnel. Former searchlight control tower replaced with wireless radio cabin. Wireless cabin fitted on mainmast platform. Two 21in. torpedo tubes removed. Admirals signal platform extended to accommodate signal equipment. Admirals bridge extended around forebridge. Structural modifications to the compass platform and forebridge, including a new wireless cabin, extra plating and antenna atop the spotting top. Repairs to the turbines and the lower hull were also made.
2 June 1939: Flagship of Battle Cruiser Squadron, Home Fleet. Transferred to Scapa Flow with *HMS Courageous* (aircraft carrier).
Late July-Early August 1939: Machinery and speed trials in the English Channel.
Late August 1939: Exercised with Home Fleet in northern waters off Scotland.
31 August 1939: Royal Navy mobilized for war. *Hood* departed Scapa Flow to patrol between Iceland and Faeroe Islands with *Repulse*, *Renown,* and destroyers.
3 September 1939: World War II officially began at 1100 hours.
5 September 1939: *Hood* narrowly avoids German submarine torpedo.
6 September 1939: Returned to Scapa Flow. Took on oil and provisions.
8-12 September 1939: *Hood*, *Renown*, *Belfast* & *Edinburgh* (light cruisers) plus 4 destroyers, were assigned to cover Iceland-Faeroes Gap to block German commerce raiders from entering Atlantic shipping lanes.
17 September 1939: Visited by Winston Churchill, 1st Lord of the Admiralty.
22-23 September 1939: Covered raid in North Sea with no action. Returned to Scapa Flow.
25-27 September 1939: At sea with *Nelson*, *Rodney* (battleships), *Repulse*, *Ark Royal* (aircraft carrier), a cruiser squadron and destroyers to provide distant cover for rescue of damaged submarine *HMS Spearfish* from North Sea. One 500lb bomb from a German bomber hit *Hood* on her port side and detonated in the sea. This caused minor flooding, but steam condenser damaged was significant. Returned to Scapa Flow.
27 September-1 October 1939: At Scapa Flow. Minor repairs made, but condenser damage unrepaired.
8 October 1939: Departed Scapa Flow with *Repulse*, and *Aurora*, *Sheffield* (light cruisers) and four destroyers towards Norwegian coast to intercept *KM Gneisenau* (battleship), *Köln* (light cruiser) and nine German destroyers reported there.
11 October 1939: Returned after interception of German task force was unsuccessful.
15-22 October 1939: On patrol between Scotland and Iceland, covering armed merchant cruisers of Northern Patrol with *Nelson*, *Rodney*, *Furious* (aircraft carrier), *Aurora*, *Belfast* and nine destroyers.
23-31 October 1939: On patrol off Norway with *Nelson*, *Rodney* and six destroyers. Covered Narvik iron ore convoy. Force was unsuccessfully attacked by *U-56*, with two torpedoes striking *Nelson*, both failing to detonate.
2-9 November 1939: Again on patrol off Norway with *Nelson*, covering Scandinavian convoy.
11-25 November 1939: Plymouth for minor repairs only.
25 November 1939: Departed on an unsuccessful intercept on what was presumed to be *KM Deutschland* (heavy cruiser), but was actually *KM Scharnhorst* and *Gneisenau* (battleships) after their sinking of *HMS Rawalpindi* (armed merchant cruiser).
29 November-2 December 1939: *Hood* and destroyers, with French warships *Dunkerque* (battlecruiser), *George Leygues*, *Montcalm* (light cruisers) and 2 destroyers, under French command, patrol the area south of Iceland to intercept German raiders. Enemy was not sighted. Returned to England.
2-11 December 1939: *Hood* on patrol with four destroyers north of Faeroe Islands.
13-17 December 1939: On patrol in North Sea with *Warspite*, *Barham* (battleships) and six destroyers to intercept *Leipzig*, *Nürnberg*, *Köln* (light cruisers) and five destroyers, but was rerouted to cover Canadian troop convoy across Atlantic Ocean to England.
23-24 December 1939: *Hood*, and *Edinburgh* and *Glasgow* (light cruisers) covers convoy carrying weapons to Finland.
27 December-5 January 1940: On patrol in North Atlantic and off Norway with four destroyers.
15-24 January 1940: At sea with *Warspite* and 8th Destroyer Flotilla patrolling the Shetland–Faeroes Gap.
9-22 February 1940: Another patrol with *Warspite* and eight destroyers, covering Scandinavian convoys and to support the boarding of the *KM Altmark* (supply ship) to free POWs, if necessary.
23 February 1940: *Hood* en route to the Clyde with *Rodney* and eight destroyers.
24 February-2 March 1940: At the Clyde. Only minor repairs accomplished.
2-7 March 1940: At sea with *Valiant* (battleship) and six destroyers to cover Norwegian convoys patrol.
7-14 March 1940: At Scapa Flow.
11 March 1940: Flag of Battle Cruiser Squadron transferred to *Renown*.
30 March 1940: Departed for Plymouth, escorted by three destroyers.
4 April-23 May 1940: At Plymouth for a refit and modernization, retubing of condensers, and many other neglected repairs. All 5.5in. secondary guns removed, with two foremost batteries plated over. Three additional 4in twin AA mounts fitted, one at the end of the shelter deck, with the other two just forward, P & S. Five UP AA mounts fitted, one atop the B turret, two abreast the forward funnel P & S, and two between the aft funnel and the mainmast P & S. Splinter shielding on all twin 4in and UP AA mounts. The 15ft. rangefinder on the control top was converted to a main armament director. Numerous Carley floats added and a degaussing cable fitted to the entire length of the hull P & S.
27 May-12 June 1940: At Liverpool for additional repairs in Gladstone Dock.
12-16 June 1940: Return to sea with *HMCS Skeena*, *Restigouche* and *St Laurent* (destroyers) to cover the ANZAC Troop Convoy aboard *Queen Mary*, *Empress of Britain*, *Aquitania*, *Mauretania*, *Andes* and *Empress of Canada* (ocean liners) from the Bay of Biscay to the Clyde. Escort reinforced by *HMS Argus* (aircraft carrier), *Dorsetshire*, *Shropshire*, *Cumberland* (heavy cruisers) and nine destroyers.

16-18 June 1940: Docked at Greenock. *Hood* resupplied and repainted.
18-23 June 1940: Escorted to Gibraltar by five destroyers, joined by *Ark Royal.*
25 June 1940: France signed an armistice with Germany. Great Britain concerned about French fleet falling into German control.
26-27 June 1940: At sea with Force H from Gibraltar, including *Ark Royal* and five destroyers to intercept French *Richelieu* (battleship), reported steaming from Dakar, and to escort her if possible, to Gibraltar. *Richelieu* returned to Dakar after meeting *HMS Dorsetshire* (heavy cruiser).
28 June-2 July 1940: At Gibraltar.
2-4 July 1940: Force H, consisting of *Ark Royal, Valiant, Resolution* (battleship), *Arethusa, Enterprise* (light cruisers), and 11 destroyers, participate in "Operation Catapult", neutralization of French fleet at Oran/Mers-el Kebir, Algeria. At 1755 to 1804hrs, Force H shells French fleet in harbor. *Bretagne* (battleship) blows up and serious damage to *Dunkerque* and *Provence* (battleship) and a cruiser. At 1809 to 1812hrs, French shore batteries engaged, allowing *Strasbourg* (battlecruiser) to escape. French suffered heavy losses, four capital ships neutralized and over 1,300 crewmen dead. British fleet suffered only light casualties, *Hood* with two slightly wounded crewmen. Unsuccessfully attacked by French bombers while returning to Gibraltar.
5-6 July 1940: *Hood*, part of Force H, returned to Mers-el-Kebir with *Ark Royal, Valiant, Arethusa, Enterprise* and 10 destroyers as "Operation Lever", and used an air strike against *Dunkerque* caused her to be beached. Returned to Gibraltar.
8-11 July 1940: Steamed again with Force H, *Ark Royal, Valiant, Resolution, Arethusa, Enterprise, Delhi,* and 10 destroyers on a diversionary attack against an Italian airfield on Sardinia while two convoys sail from Malta to Alexandria. Attacked by Italian bombers with several near misses but no hits. Sardinia mission aborted, but both convoys arrived safely. Returned to Gibraltar.
27 July 1940: While reloading UP mounting on B turret, three crewmen badly burnt when weapon accidentally fires off 20 charges over Gibraltar Harbor.
31 July-4 August 1940: Steamed with Force H, *Ark Royal, Valiant, Resolution, Enterprise,* and nine destroyers for an attack on Sardinian airfield while *HMS Argus* (aircraft carrier) flew off replacement aircraft for Malta. Attacked by Italian bombers with no damage. Returned to Gibraltar.
4 August 1940: Briefly at Gibraltar for refueling. Departed same day with *Ark Royal, Valiant, Arethusa, Enterprise,* and nine destroyers for Scapa Flow.
10 August 1940: Flagship duties for Force H transferred to *Renown.* Flagship, Battle Cruiser Squadron, Home Fleet duties transferred to *Hood.*
16-24 August 1940: At Rosyth for replacement of A turret's port 15in. gun. Transferred to Scapa Flow.
13 September 1940: Departed for Rosyth with *Nelson, Rodney,* and *Bonaventure, Naiad, Cairo* (light cruisers), and seven destroyers against possible German invasion. Returned to Rosyth.
28-29 September 1940: At sea with *Naiad* to intercept enemy cruiser and convoy reported off Norway. Returned to Scapa Flow.
15-19 October 1940: At sea off Norway with five destroyers to cover Force D, consisting of *HMS Furious* (aircraft carrier), *Berwick* and *Norfolk* (heavy cruisers), attacking German warships at Tromsö, Norway. Returned to Scapa Flow.
23–24 October 1940: Sortie with *Repulse,* and *Dido, Phoebe* (light cruisers), and three destroyers on reported enemy movement. Returned to Scapa Flow after no contact with enemy forces.
28-31 October 1940: Again at sea with *Repulse, Furious* and six destroyers to intercept enemy commerce raider reported in North Atlantic. Returned to Scapa Flow after no contact with enemy forces.
5-11 November 1940: Departed Scapa Flow with *Repulse, Dido, Naiad, Bonaventure,* and six destroyers to intercept *KM Admiral Scheer* (heavy cruiser) reported on return to Brest, or Lorient after sinking *HMS Jervis Bay* (armed merchant cruiser) and attacking convoy HX84. Returned to Scapa Flow with no contact.
23-29 November 1940: At sea with seven destroyers covering minelaying operations in Denmark Strait. During this, *Hood's* radio direction finding hut on mainmast gutted by fire. Returned to Scapa Flow.
12 December 1940: Near mutiny by some of the crew over lack of pay and leave.
18-20 December 1940: Return to sea for exercises with *Nelson, Repulse*, and *Nigeria, Edinburgh, Manchester,* and *Aurora* (light cruisers), and numerous destroyers south-west of Faeroe Islands. Returned to Scapa Flow.
24-29 December 1940: *Hood* at sea with *Edinburgh* and four destroyers to form patrol in Iceland-Faeroes gap against passage of *KM Admiral Hipper* (heavy cruiser). Enemy not sighted, returned to Scapa Flow.
2-5 January 1941: At sea with four destroyers covering minelaying operations around Faeroe Islands. Returned to Scapa Flow.
11-13 January 1941: Departed with *Repulse,* and *Edinburgh, Birmingham* (light cruisers), and six destroyers to cover two large convoys against suspected German surface raiders. Returned to Rosyth.
13 January-18 March 1941: While at Rosyth, *Hood* unloaded all ammunition and underwent a refit. Modifications included addition of Type 284 main armament fire control radar, removal of the forward topmast, fitting a yard to the rear of the forward starfish platform, foremast torpedo lookout removed, HF/DF equipment and wireless cabin removed from mainmast, steam picket boats replaced by 35ft motor launches and blades of starboard turbine replaced.
18-23 March 1941: Rendezvoused with *Queen Elizabeth, Nelson,* and *London* (heavy cruiser), and six destroyers to intercept *KM Scharnhorst* and *Gneisenau* 200 miles SW of Faeroe Islands. Later joined by *HMS King George V* (battleship), between Iceland and the Faeroe Islands. Enemy not sighted, returned to Scapa Flow with *Queen Elizabeth* and four destroyers.
28 March-6 April 1941: *Hood* at sea with three destroyers to escort convoy HX118 from Halifax, Nova Scotia, but diverted to Bay of Biscay with *Nigeria* and *Fiji* (light cruisers) to assist Force H against breakout of *KM Scharnhorst* and *Gneisenau* from Brest. *Hood's* task force relieved by *King George V* and *London* and retuned to Scapa Flow.
6 April-14 April 1941: At Scapa Flow, returned with three destroyers briefly to refuel. Resumed patrol in Bay of Biscay against breakout of *KM Scharnhorst* and *Gneisenau* from Brest.
14-18 April 1941: Returned to Scapa Flow.
18 April 1941: Departed again for Bay of Biscay with *Kenya* (light cruiser) and three destroyers to resume patrol off Brest.
19 April 1941: Altered course for Norwegian waters following reports that *KM Bismarck* (battleship) had left Kiel and was heading north-west with two *Leipzig*-class light cruisers and three destroyers.
21 April 1941: Diverted to Hvalfjord, Iceland, with one destroyer against breakout of *KM Bismarck* into Atlantic.
26 April 1941: At Hvalfjord, assists in repair of *HMS Scimitar* (destroyer).
28 April-3 May 1941: Put to sea with *Suffolk, Norfolk,* and four destroyers to cover two convoys against German surface raiders. Returned to Hvalfjord.
4 May 1941: Departed Hvalfjord for Scapa Flow with

four destroyers.
6-20 May 1941: At Scapa Flow. While there, *Hood* conducted range and inclination exercises with *King George V*. Based on intelligence reports that *KM Bismarck* was likely to attempt a break-out into the Atlantic, all ships of the Home Fleet were on alert.
21 May 1941: *Hood, Prince of Wales* (battleship), and six destroyers departed for Hvalfjord at 2356hrs.
22 May 1941: *Hood's* task force ordered to proceed to waters off southern Iceland due to information that *KM Bismarck* and a heavy cruiser (*Prinz Eugen*) had departed Norway. From this position they would be able to cover both the Denmark Strait and the Iceland-Faeroes Gap.
23 May 1941:
1922hrs: *Bismarck* and *Prinz Eugen* sighted by *Suffolk* in Denmark Strait. *Suffolk* ducked into fog bank and radioed sighting, shadowed German warships using radar.
2031hrs: German warships sight *Norfolk* and open fire, but British ship was able to escape into fog bank, later joining *Suffolk*.
2352hrs: *Suffolk* loses contact with German ships.
24 May 1941:
0200hrs: Daybreak. *Hood* task force on course to intercept German ships southwest of Iceland. Escorting destroyers dispatched to search due north.
0246hrs: *Suffolk* regained contact with German ships.
0535hrs: German ships sighted by *Prince of Wales* at a distance of over 17 nautical miles. Germans sighted smoke from both British ships, but believed it to be from a single cruiser.
0537hrs: British turned to 40° starboard to close range.
0543hrs: Germans saw two distinct ships on an intercept course but were still unable to positively identify types.
0549hrs: VADM Holland, noting that Germans may have turned away, ordered his force to turn 20° to starboard to close range once again.
0552.5hrs: *Hood* opened fire on lead German ship, *Prinz Eugen*, believing it to be *Bismarck*. After two or three salvoes, *Hood* switches to *Bismarck*.
0553hrs: *Prince of Wales* correctly identifies and fires upon rear ship, *Bismarck*. By this point, Germans understood it was impossible to avoid an engagement and turned south to meet British.
0555hrs: British ships turned 20° to port together in an attempt to bring their rear turrets to bear. At the same time, *Bismarck* opened fire on *Hood* at a range of 12.5 miles and closing. *Prinz Eugen's* first salvo followed shortly thereafter. Germans concentrated fire on *Hood* from start and were immediately on target. British, meanwhile, had initially divided their fire. *Prince of Wales* also had mechanical problems. This reduced the odds of scoring effective hits quickly. Despite this, *Prince of Wales* hit *Bismarck* three times within first seven minutes of battle.
0557hrs: *Prinz Eugen* struck *Hood* amidships with her second salvo and started a fire in the 4in. AA and UP rocket ammunition. *Bismarck* may also have struck *Hood* at this time, as bodies were seen falling from *Hood's* spotting top.
0559hrs: *Prinz Eugen* ordered to switch target to *Prince of Wales*. *Bismarck* continued to engage *Hood* with her main armament.
0600hrs: British ships altered course another 20° to port in order to quickly bring her after turrets to bear. During commencement of turn, *Hood's* after turrets were brought to bear, and one or more of them fired. At this time, *Hood* was straddled by *Bismarck's* fifth salvo. One or more shells were observed to strike *Hood* between the mainmast and X turret. After a slight delay, a massive sheet of flame erupted from engine room vents around the mainmast and shot skyward nearly one thousand feet. This was quickly followed by a huge explosion which immediately obscured *Hood* from view, with dense clouds of black and yellow smoke billowing high into the sky. Within the smoke column, multiple small flashes and fireballs were seen. At same time, a multitude of debris rained back down upon *Hood* and the surrounding water. In less than one minute, the separated stern slowed to a stop, tilted forward, and sank rapidly. The forward two-thirds of *Hood* continued ahead a short distance and then came to a stop. The bow settled, and rose nearly to vertical as it twisted to port and sank in under three minutes. Of *Hood's* crew, only 3 escape alive.
0601hrs: *Prince of Wales* executed evasive maneuver to avoid collision with wreckage of *Hood*. She passed the *Hood* as the forward section sank not more than one-half mile distant. Meantime, the German ships switched fire to *Prince of Wales*, scoring seven hits.
0602hrs: *Prince of Wales*, moderately damaged and outgunned, turned away from German ships, making smoke, and withdrew from the engagement.
0609hrs: Both sides ceased fire.
0615hrs: *Norfolk*, 14 miles astern of battle area, transmitted loss of *Hood* to Royal Navy Headquarters.
0637hrs: *Norfolk* transmitted *Hood's* sinking location to RN destroyers to search for survivors, as she could not stop her distant shadow of the German task force.
0745hrs: Destroyers *Electra* and *Echo* arrived at the location of *Hood's* sinking to find only three survivors. Search continues, joined by four other destroyers.
0920hrs: Search called off with no other survivors located. *Electra* transports survivors to Hvalfjord, Iceland.

July 2001: Expedition led by underwater explorer David Mearns, in collaboration with Channel 4 Television, located the wreck of *HMS Hood*.

November 2001: *Hood* recommended for recognition by British government as a war grave and a "Protected Place".

The images on the following page are all of the Hood *under construction at the John Brown Shipyard at Clydebank. The top left photo is of the very early stages of the construction of the keel, while the bottom right photo is of the final stages of construction just prior to launching.*

Hood *on the slipway, just prior to launch. On this and the following four pages are views of the hull plating detail. Also, note that the main armor belt was not installed at that time. The stress upon a hull at the time of launch was severe, and the weight of the armor would have made it so. The side armor was installed soon after launch, during the fitting out phase of the ship's construction. Close inspection of the photos in this sequence will reveal the riveted construction, standard at that time. In the small inset photograph, the large stacks of chain bundled up were attached to the vessel and used to slow the hull as it entered the water. The shipyard personnel in the image give a good idea as to the sheer size of this ship. Note the underwater torpedo tube door in the photo as marked. One was fitted both port and starboard, asymmetrically.*

This image to the right is of the Hood *prior to launch. The shape of the anti-torpedo blister on the exterior of the hull is visible forward of the propellers in this photograph.*

An aerial view of the John Brown Shipyard *during the final construction phase of the hull of the* Hood.

The photograph on this and the previous page are of the stern area of the massive hull of the Hood, *showing the rudder and the propellers. To have an idea of the size, the rudder was 26ft. long and 18ft. tall. The propellers were about 15ft. in diameter and were cast from bronze in one piece.*

On August 22, 1918, the Hood *was launched. At that time, and for quite sometime thereafter, she would be the largest warship built. At that time, she was completed up to the main deck, with only part of her machinery installed and none of her armament and very little of her superstructure fitted. Her launch weight, almost 22,000 tons, was as great, or greater than the displacement of some fully loaded warships then in service. In the photo to the left and above, the ledge upon which the main side armor belt was to be installed is visible. As with the photos prior to the launch, portions of the hull plating detail are visible in the area of the bow in the image to the left.*

The image to the right, on the next page, is of the Hood *during the fitting out phase of her construction. The photo was taken on December 2, 1919, at the John Brown Shipyard. Construction is well along, as the superstructure is almost complete. The forward main armament of 15in. guns was in the process of installation.*

The image on the previous page and above were taken on January 9, 1920, at the John Brown Shipyard. As that shipbuilder was under a tight schedule to complete much-needed merchant vessels, the Hood *was to have her final fitting out at HM Dockyard, Rosyth. The photos on these pages and the next seven are all from the same date, showing the ship under preparation to leave Clydebank for Rosyth.*

Hood *was painted at this time with paint #AP507A Dark Gray on all vertical surfaces and the steel decks. The wood decks were natural teak. The bridge decks were covered with a linoleum called Corticene, which had a reddish-brown color. Note that the linoleum used by many navies of the world at that time was very simular in color due to the manufacturing processes and the materials used.*

This is an aerial view of the shelter deck of the Hood, *where the ships boats were stowed. Also in this image is the single 5.5in. shielded secondary armament, which mounted only on the* Hood, *the light battlecruiser* Furious *and the light cruisers* Birkenhead *and* Chester.

Note the above-water torpedo tube doors to the lower right area of the above photograph.

The two images on this page are of the after portion of the ship. The upper photo is of the shelter deck with the mainmast and the after control position. Also seen here are the single 4in. HA (high angle) AA (anti-aircraft) guns. The lower photo is of the after main armament and the stern. In the British Royal Navy, the main armament gun turrets were designated as follows; with the Hood, *the two forward turrets were labeled as A and B, while the after turrets were X and Y. Some ships of the Royal Navy had more than four turrets, as was the case with the* HMS Againcourt, *which had more than any other capital ship ever built. The seven centerline mounted turrets of the* Againcourt *were named after the days of the week, starting at the bow with Monday.*

This photograph is another view of the shelter deck, known by the crew as the boat deck, and the 5.5in. secondary gun battery, this time from the starboard side. There are yard workers visible in this image who give scale to the size of this massive warship.

Another starboard side view, this time from the dock, looking at the funnels, as the forward boilers are raising steam for the Hood's *voyage to Rosyth for completion of the fitting out phase of construction.*

Three more views of the Hood *from the starboard side, taken from the dock as she raises steam on January 9, 1920. These images are of the area around the funnels and the bridge. The piping around the bridge structure were the various voice tubes for communicating throughout the ship. The size of the conning tower is also evident in these photos.*

This photograph is a closeup of the image on page 18. It is of the shelter deck with the boat stowage visible. Note the style of the vents on the deck. Also, note the design of the boat stowage cradles. The wood-covered portion of the shelter deck runs forward to the large vent to the extreme right of this image.

Hood *being pulled away from the dock at the John Brown Shipyard, at Clydebank, January 9, 1920. The warship was being transferred to HM Dockyard, Rosyth. While en route,* Hood *went through some preliminary trials in the Firth of Clyde.*

The two images on this page, and the title page, are of Hood *during her voyage to Rosyth, in the Firth of Clyde, on preliminary trials. During this voyage, a force 8 gale was blowing. This was truly an extreme weather condition to run a vessel on its trials. This trial also showed that the* Hood *would be a "wet" ship, as the additional armor made the ship ride lower in the water, causing her to ship a fair amount of water over the bow, while the fantail was almost always awash in moderate weather.*

The two photographs on the previous page are of the HMS Hood, *just after commissioning into the Royal Navy. Her massive size and graceful form would draw crowds at every port of call she put into.*

The above image illustrates the expanse of the shelter deck. The gun in the foreground is one of the ships 4in. AA weapons. The ammunition for the gun was stowed in the locker at the extreme lower right of the image.

Foredeck of the Hood, *soon after commissioning. The wooden deck planking was 9 inches in width. That was much larger than that cut for other navies. Generally, other navies employed deck planking about 4, 5, or even 6 inches in width. This was laid down on top of the steel weather deck, acting as an insulator and anti-skid.*

Forecastle, H.M.S. "Hood."

Another view of the shelter deck of the Hood. *The size of the funnels was very large to accommodate the amount of exhaust from the massive propulsion system (24 boilers) to make the largest warship in the world steam at a top speed of 32 knots. The large pipes attached to the sides of the funnels were used to discharge excess steam.*

The photograph on the left is closeup of the forward main gun turrets and the bridge structure. The design of the gun turrets on the Hood *was unique. Note the tampions in the muzzle of the main gun barrels. They have the crest of the* Hood *family.*

The image to the right is of the foredeck, viewed from up on the bridge structure, probably from the searchlight platform in the center of the image on the left. The aircraft flying-off platform is visible in its stowed condition atop the B turret. The large box-like items backing the forward breakwater are for paravane stowage.

This photograph is of the Hood *during her "Empire", or "World Cruise", at the port of Wellington, New Zealand, April 24 to May 8, 1924. She was with the battlecruiser* HMS Repulse *and the First Light Cruiser Squadron, consisting of* HMS Danae, Dauntless, Dragon, Delhi *and* Dunedin, *on a world tour of all of the British Commonwealth countries and other friendly ports of call.* Hood *and the accompanying warships steamed 38,152 miles and visited numerous foreign countries around the world. Over one million people visited the entire British Squadron, with 752,049 people having visited the* Hood *alone.*

ROYAL NAVY BATTLECRUISER

H. M. S. HOOD

May 1941

Illustration by Thomas Schmid

Two additional views of the Hood *at both Wellington and Aukland, New Zealand. This was the largest warship to visit the small island nation at that time. Above is a view of the bridge structure. The maze of piping running under the platforms is part of the extensive system of voice pipes. The warship was kept very pristine during this tour, as seen in this series of photographs. Note the range dials mounted both port and starboard above the small searchlight platform on the tripod mast. These were to communicate the distance to target to a ship steaming in column ahead of* Hood.

HMS Hood *at the docks in Honolulu, Hawaii, June 11, 1924. She has rigged her canvas awnings to provide some comfort from the sun in the summer months for the multitude of visitors. Her stay at Honolulu was from June 6th to the 12th.*

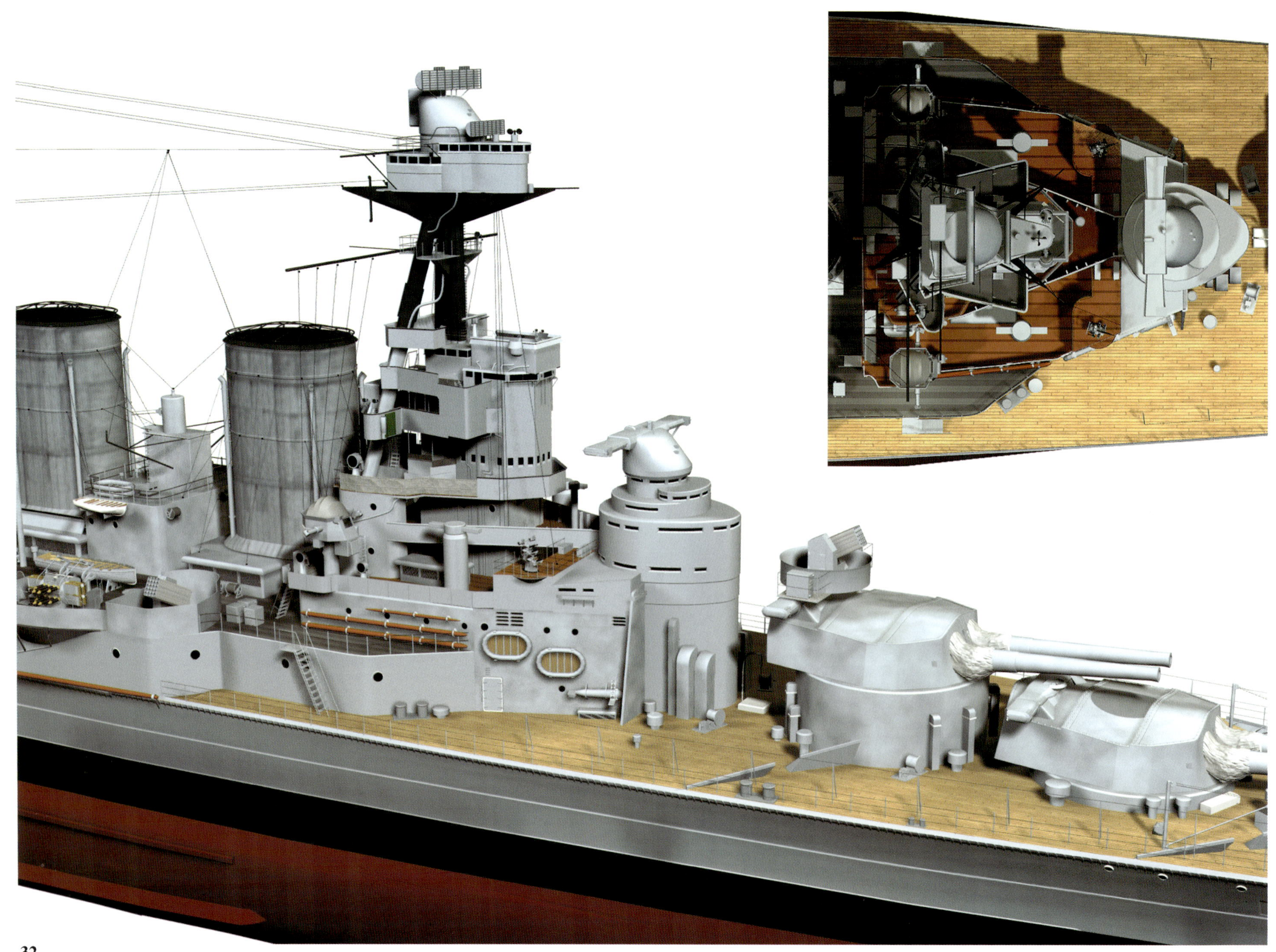

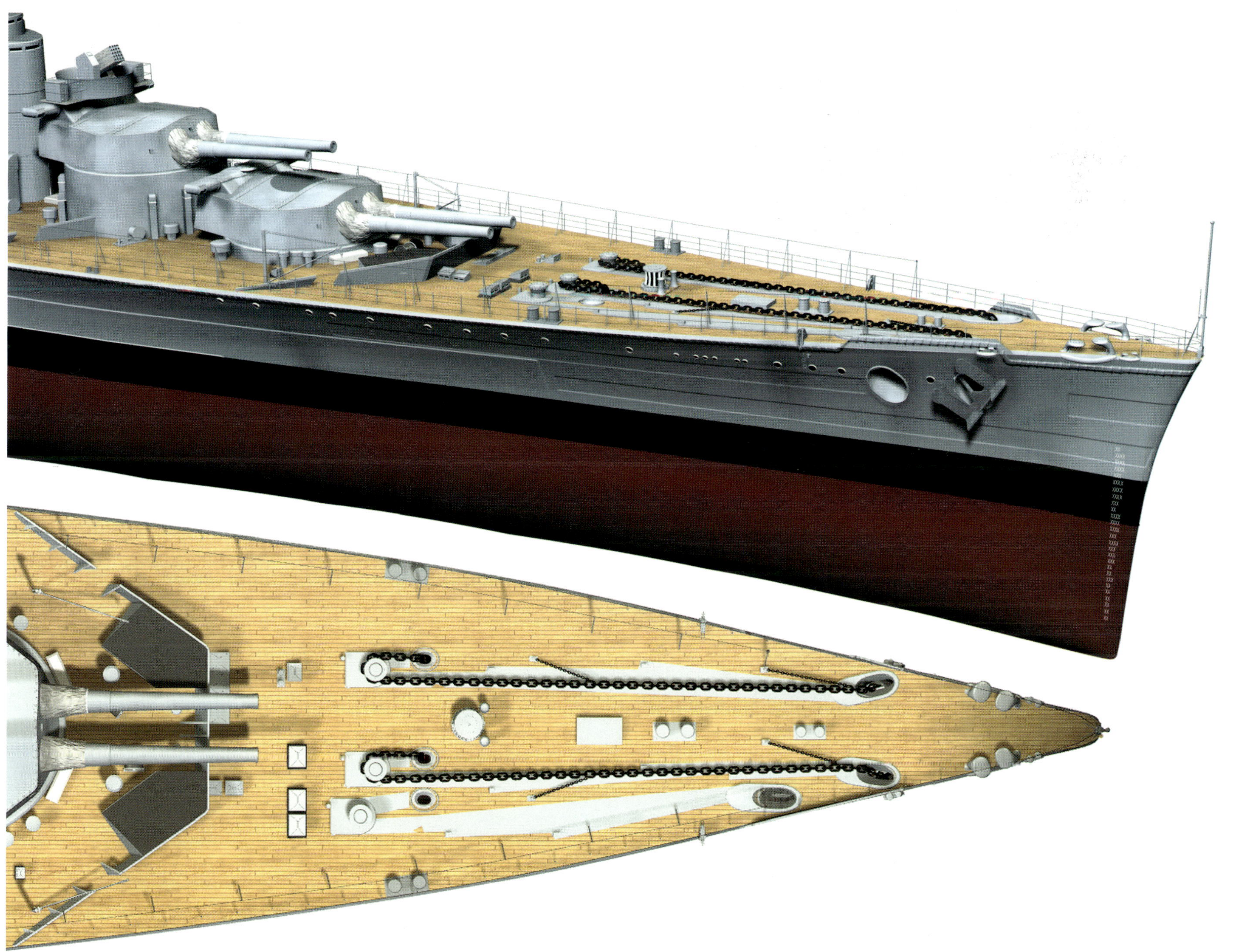

The photograph on this and the previous page are enlarged images of the photo on page 34. This aerial view provides a layout of the ship rarely seen, especially at this date in time. In the photo on the left, the rangefinder in the extreme right of the image is the midships torpedo control tower. Also, in this same photograph, about the center of the image, is where the wooden plank sheathing atop the shelter deck is separated from the bare steel deck forward by an expansion joint and runs to the left.

ROYAL NAVY BATTLECRUISER

H. M. S. HOOD

May 1941

Illustrations by Thomas Schmid

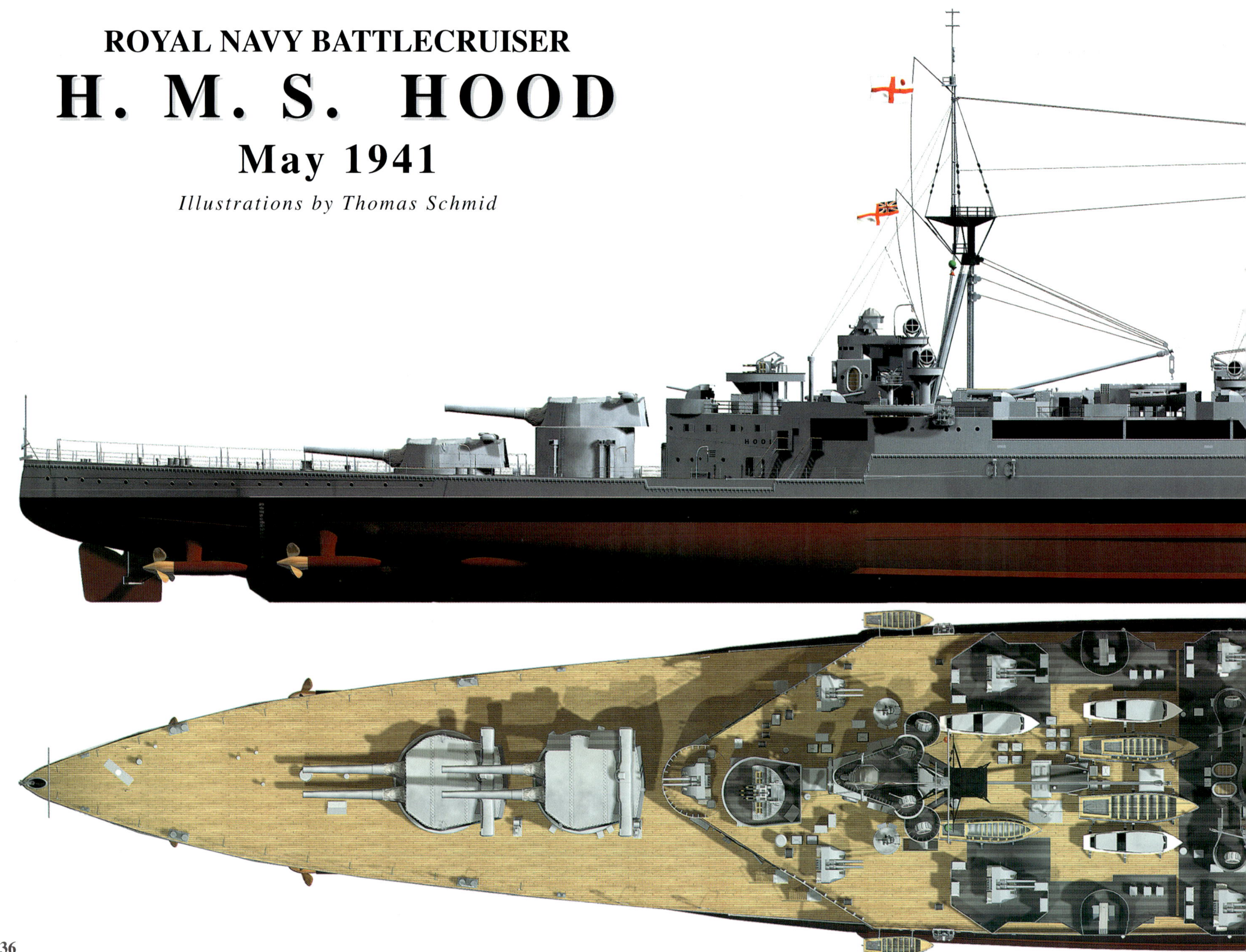

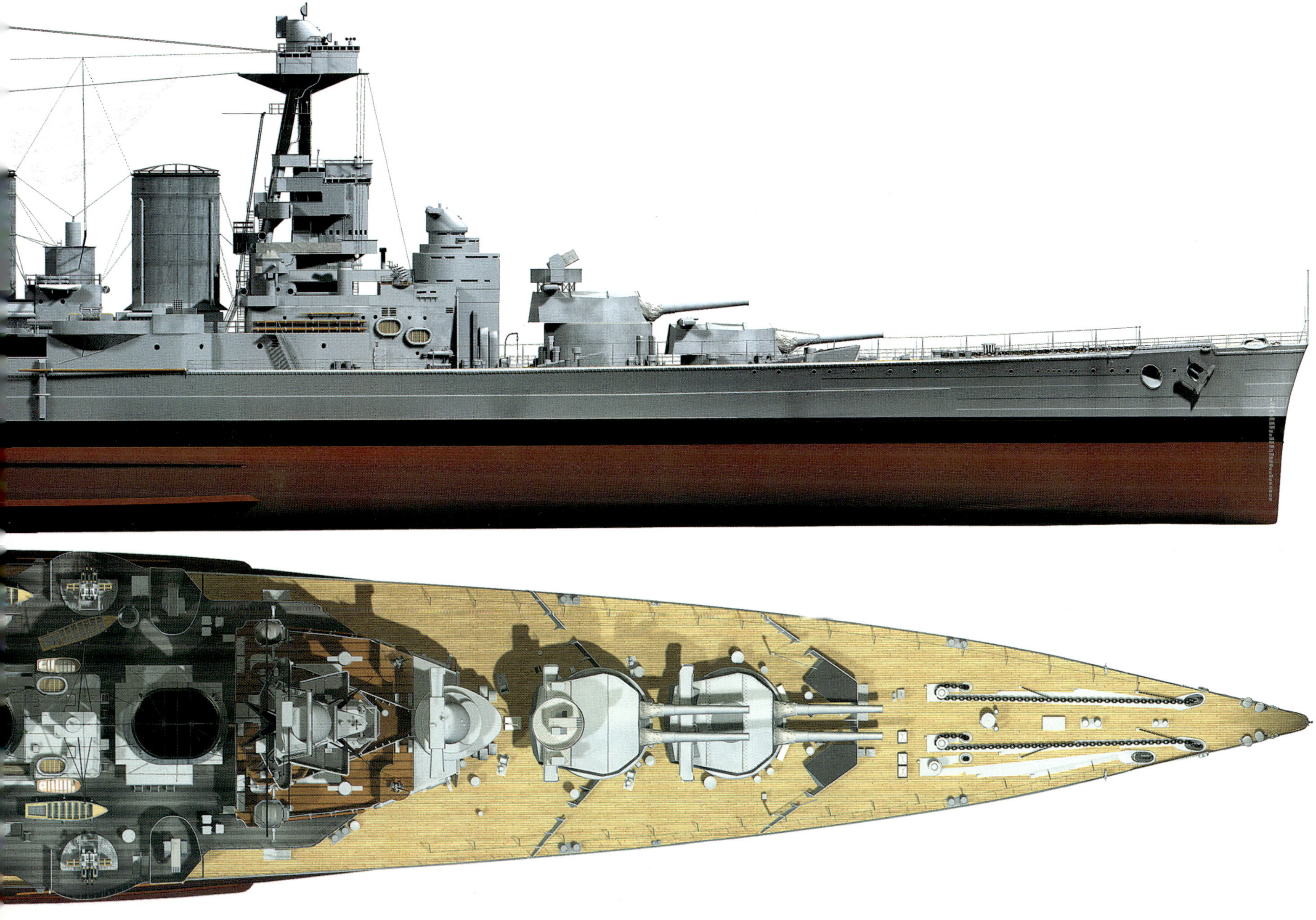

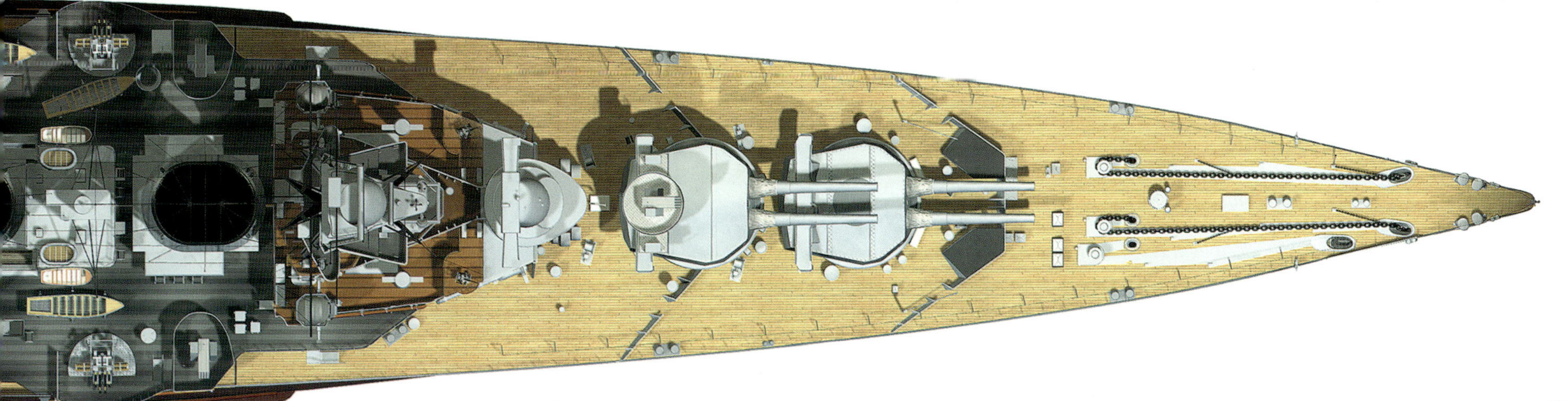

The photographs on this, the following page, and pages 42 and 43, are all of HMS Hood *as she departed Hawaiian waters, en route to Victoria, Vancouver Island, British Columbia, Canada. These were all taken by a US Navy aerial reconnaissance aircraft. The image above is of the British warship just as she is leaving the harbor area at Honolulu. She still had much of her tropical awnings deployed at this time.*

The image on the following page was a much closer fly-over, showing much more of the details from an aerial perspective. The large flag flying at the top of the foremast is that of Vice Admiral Sir Frederick Laurence Field. Note the variety of the ships boats carried amidships. At the time this image was taken, Hood *carried the following boats; two 50ft. steam pinnace, a 45ft. Admirals barge, two 35ft. motor boats, a 16ft. fast motor dinghy, two 42ft. launches, four 32ft. cutters, two, or three 30ft. sailing gigs, two 27ft. whalers and two 16ft. dinghies.*

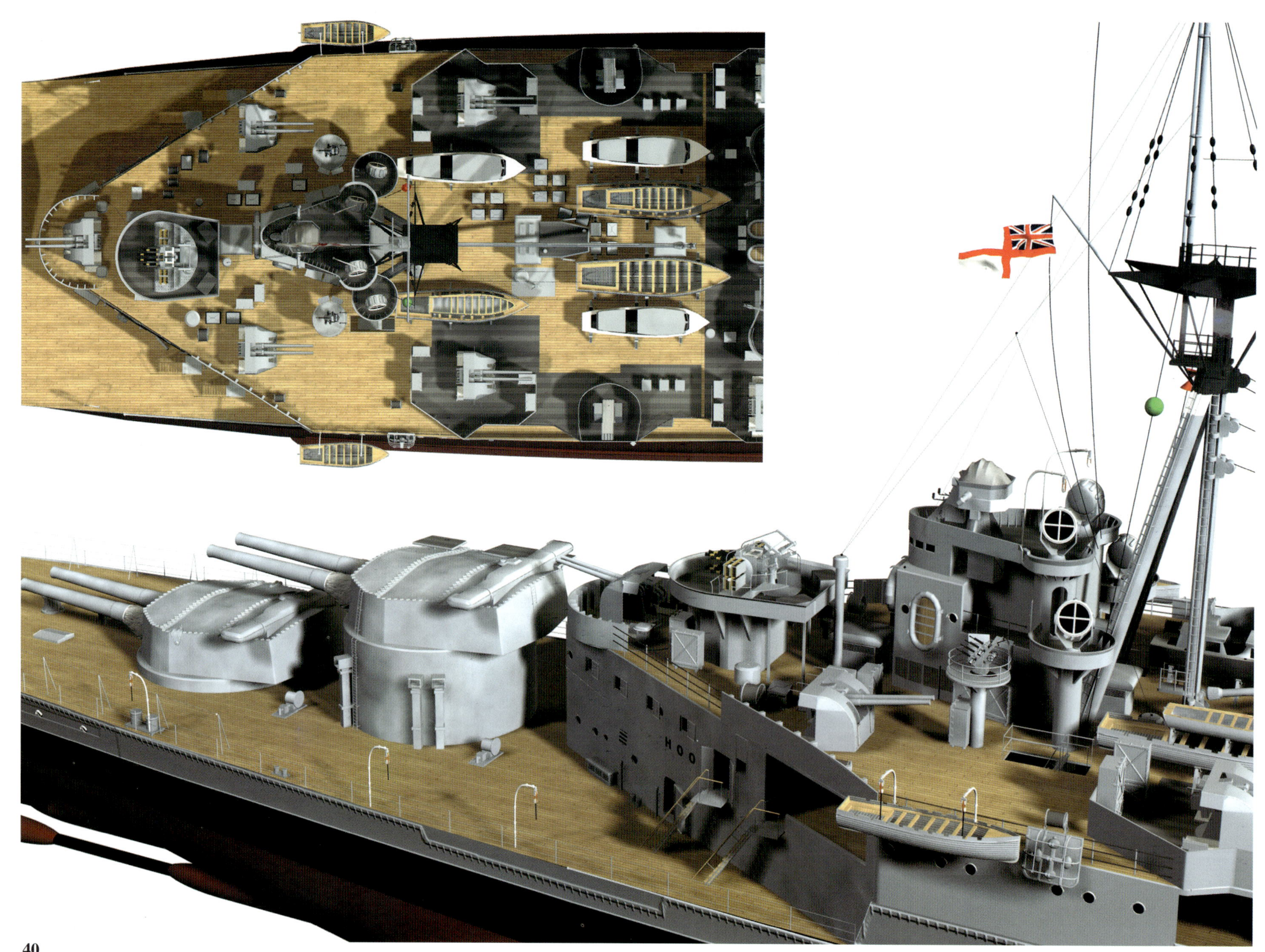

Another in the series of photographs taken while the Hood *was departing Hawaiian waters on June 12, 1924. This next leg of her "World Cruise" to Canada was almost 2,500 miles, which she would cover in a leisurely eight days. The very large armored director atop the conning tower housed a 30ft. rangefinder and was used for main battery control.*

The exceptionally tall mainmast on the Hood *was a common sight on capital warship in the 1920s. The reason for this was that radio at that time operated on low power and needed a very tall antenna to gain better reception. The majority of the rigging lines off of the mast were in fact the radio antennae.*

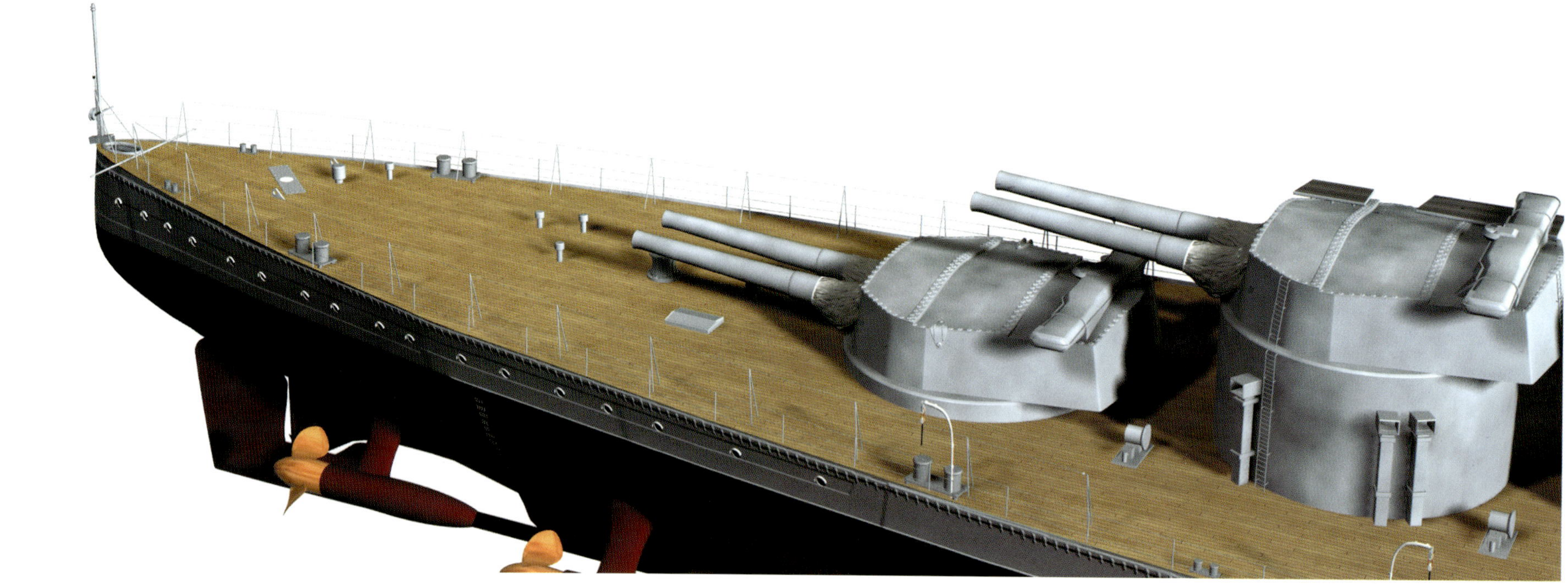

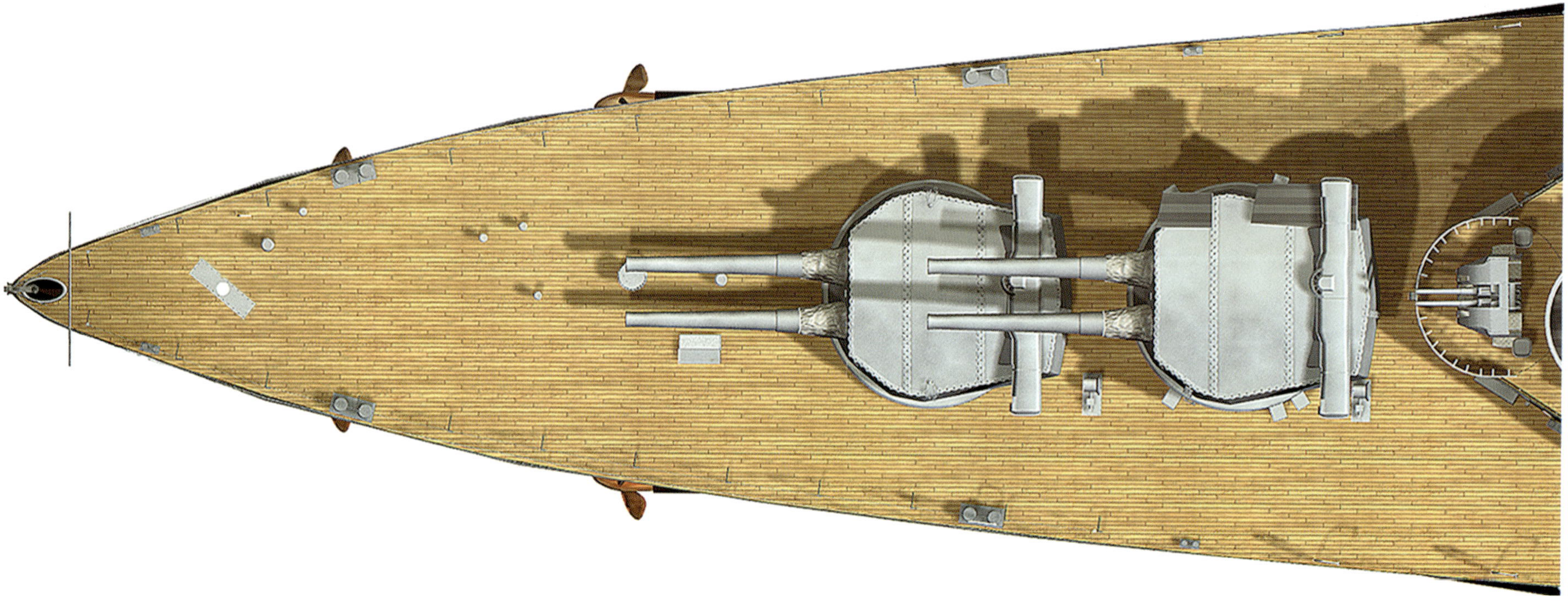

Hood, *at San Francisco, California, United States, 7 to 11 July, 1924. To honor the county of the port of call, the national flag, this time the "Stars and Stripes" of the United States of America, was flown from the foremast. One of the ship's single 4in. AA guns appears in the foreground of the right hand photo. The small circular items in the rigging on either side of the American flag are insulators for the various radio antenna wires.*

Another view of the Hood *at San Francisco, California. Note the rings painted on the gun barrels of the B turret. These were the location markers for each of the support struts for the aircraft flying off platform when fully extended the length of the gun barrels. As can be seen in this photograph, she was open for tours to the American public at that time.*

HMS Hood *about to pass out of one of the locks in the Panama Canal. She is transiting from the Pacific to the Atlantic Ocean, still on the "World Tour," in company with the battlecruiser* HMS Repulse. *As with most of the places these massive warships visited, they drew huge crowds.* Hood *and* Repulse *transited the canal on July 23 and 24, 1924, the light cruisers having parted company and steamed south to visit countries along the Pacific coast of South America.*

Both of the photographs on this page are close-up views of the Hood *while transiting the Panama Canal. With her beam at 105ft., the passage of the canal was a tight fit, as the Gatun Locks in the image to the left were only 110ft. wide each. The three locks raised the* Hood *85ft. above sea level.*

Royal Marines muster on deck during the passage through the Panama Canal.

The two images on this and the main photo on the following page were all taken while the Hood *was transiting the Panama Canal in July 1924.*

The small inset photo on the following page is of the battle-cruiser off the East Coast of the United States in 1924.

The fee for the Hood *to transit the Panama Canal at that time was a little more than $22,000.00. This few varied with the tonnage of the ship.*

The after turrets of the Hood *are pictured here during battle practice off of Portland, England, in August 1926. The quarterdeck on the* Hood *was quite often awash when the ship was running at high speed in anything other than a dead calm. In these two photos, the X and Y turrets were both trained on their extreme forward bearing. The steel portion of the aircraft flying-off platform is visible atop the X turret. The warship in the background of the inset photograph is one of the* Renown-*class battlecruisers.*

This series of photographs was taken near the middle of a refit on the Hood, *during the month of June 1931. She has set out of Portsmouth on trials to test the newly fitted catapult and aircraft crane. It was at this time that the aircraft platform was removed from the X turret. On the 26th of June, during the initial testing of the aircraft operations from the* Hood, *the Fairey 3F was lost upon takeoff. The ship could carry only one aircraft for use with the catapult. It was recovered and replaced by the crane to stern of the catapult.*

During "Navy Week" each year at Portsmouth, England, a few of the British Royal Navy warships were open to the public for viewing. Here, the Hood *is being visited by civilians, sometime in the late summer of 1931.*

This view of the foredeck of the Hood *was taken on July 18, 1932. She still retained her flying-off platform atop the B turret, even though no aircraft were operated from the ship any longer. The RN had no aircraft suitable for use from the platform since the early 1920s.*

The two photographs on this page were taken on July 27, 1932. Hood *has just put into Portsmouth for repairs and a refit after fleet exercises. At that time, all of the aircraft equipment was removed as it proved very difficult to operate in anything but calm weather. The aircraft was also vulnerable to weather while in transit and to blast damage from the ship's 15in. guns. Both of the 9ft. rangefinders fitted to the Control Top were also removed during this refit. Note that the exposed portions of the anchor chain was painted white at that time.*

A posed view of Hood *with the A and B turrets trained to starboard, just after her refit in July-August 1932.*

July 16, 1935, HMS Hood *participated in the Silver Jubilee Review at Spithead.*

Another of the series of photographs of Hood *after the conclusion of the refit in 1932. Her paint was still in the AP507A Dark Gray scheme. All the canvas blast covers on the main and the secondary weapons were bleached white.*

In the drydock at Portsmouth Navy Base in February 1935 after a collision with HMS Renown *during fleet exercises. The collision actually took place on January 23rd, when the bow of* Renown *struck the* Hood *and scraped down the side to hit the propellers. Note the damage to the starboard propellers in this drydock image.*

The images on this page all date from 1935 and 1936. The paint scheme of Hood *after her June 1936 refit was in AP507C Mediterranean Light Gray, as seen in this 1937 photograph.*

The photographs above and to the right are of Hood *in the waters off of Spain during the Spanish Civil War. Note the "Neutrality Stripes" atop the B turret. The colors were red, white and blue.* Hood *operated in the Mediterranean Ocean at this time, so her vertical color was AP507C Mediterranean Light Gray, dark gray on the steel decks and all wood decks were unpainted. The image below was taken about 1938 in the Grand Harbor at Valletta, Malta. Malta at that time was a small island just south of Sicily, annexed by the British Empire in 1814 and used by the Royal Navy as a major base in the Mediterranean Ocean.*

The image to the left is another of the Hood *in the Grand Harbor at Valletta, Malta, in the late 1930s.*

The photograph at the bottom of this page was taken in early August 1939, just after the end of a major refit at Portsmouth. Her overall painting at that time had then been switched back to AP507A Dark Gray.

The small inset photograph on the left shows one of the single 4in. AA guns aboard the Hood *prior to her 1939 refit. The crewmen posing for the photo were all wearing gas masks. The warship in the background is one of the* Renown*-class battlecruisers.*

This image is an enlargement of the bridge structure at the conclusion of Hood's *refit in August 1939. She is setting out to complete compass trials, flying the flag of Vice-Admiral Whitworth.*

In the drydock at Portsmouth in June, or July, 1939 for minor maintenance, which was followed by machinery trials in the English Channel.

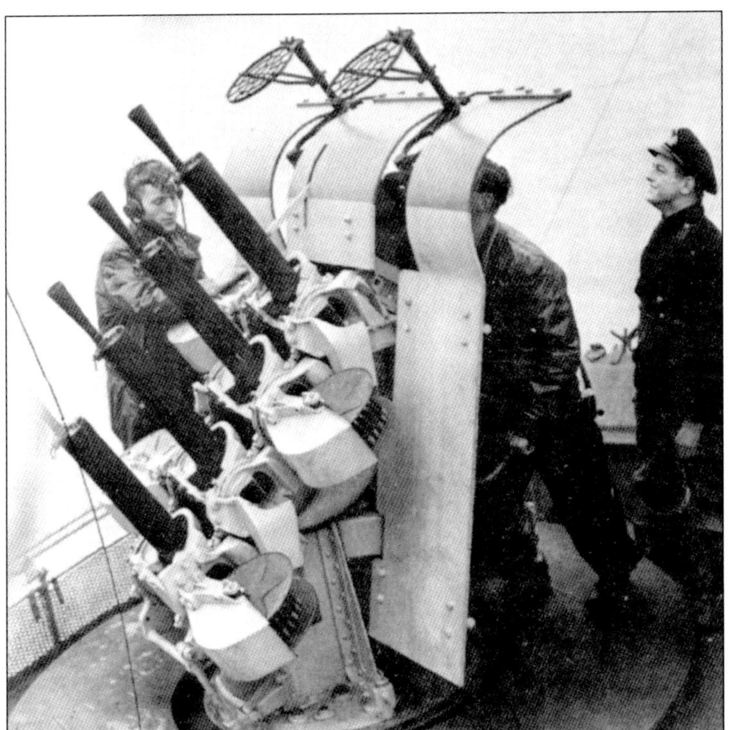

The photographs on this page are of the medium and light anti-aircraft weapons and an anti-aircraft gun director. The director was a HACS Mk. 3 with a 15ft. rangefinder. The four-barreled anti-aircraft mount in the lower left image was a quadruple 0.50in. machine gun, two of which were first fitted in 1933, another two were added in 1937 and retained until the ship was sunk. The upper and lower right images are of one of the type of 2 pounder "Pom-Pom" medium anti-aircraft weapons carried aboard the Hood. *This eight barreled weapon could through up a huge wall of protective fire. It was a 40mm bore weapon that had a combined rate of fire of up to 115rpm, carrying a total of 5,670 rounds on the mount.* Hood *carried two of these from 1931, with a third added in 1937 and retained until her loss.*

The main photograph on this page dates from October 1940, just at the completion of a refit. The Hood *lies at anchor in Scapa Flow, with the crew finishing the last of the painting of the ship in AP507B Medium Gray. The small inset photo was taken on the same day, with the battlecruiser* Repulse *in the background.*

This photograph is of the Hood *while at anchor in Scapa Flow after the completion of her March-May refit in early September 1940. She had the port gun barrel on A turret replaced the month previous at Rosyth due to cracks found in that gun. One of the additions to the warship seen in this image was the degaussing cable, visible running on the hull just below the deck edge. This was a protective measure against magnetic mines.*

The weapon in the two photos to the left was called a "UP" mount. UP stood for "Unrotated Projectile" which was a 7in. diameter rocket, filled with wire, a small charge, and a parachute. The attacking aircraft would theoretically run into the wire and detonate the charge. Hood *carried 5 of these ineffective 20 barreled weapons from 1940 onwards. There is no record of a UP weapon downing an aircraft.*

The image to the right is of the crew finishing up some of the painting of the Hood *in September 1940. The lighter color was the new coat of AP507B Medium Gray. Note the location of the ships name board, both port and starboard.*

The images on this page are of the Mk. 19 twin 4in./45cal. dual-purpose weapon, of which there were four units fitted in 1939, with an additional three more fitted in 1940. This was the primary medium caliber anti-aircraft weapon for the Royal Navy during the Second World War, fitted to most cruisers, battleships and some escort vessels, armed merchant cruisers, destroyers, aircraft carriers, and many auxiliaries as a dual-purpose mount.

The photo to the left is of the foredeck, taken from the air defense position, sometime after May 1940. The right hand image is of some of a 4in. gun crew posing on the foredeck in October 1940. Note that a wartime censor has scratched the UP launcher, mounted atop B turret, from the image.

The two photographs on this page are of the shelter deck, taken from the control top, on the after side of the tripod foremast. These images date from October 1940.

The photograph above of the foredeck awash while the warship was running at high speed was taken on March 25th, 1941. At that time, the Hood *was a very wet ship, due to her increased tonnage from additions from the many refits during her career. The bows were especially wet because of the additional bunkerage of 720 tons of fuel oil forward following her refit in 1931. The image to the right is of the forward portion of the* Hood*, taken from the extreme foredeck in April 1941. The large radar antenna atop the Control Top is for the Type 284 Gunnery Radar, installed during her January-March 1941 refit. The Royal Navy claimed the radar had an accuracy of 1500ft. @ 10 miles range, with better accuracy as the range decreased. The canvas-covered object seen just above the B turret was one of the warship's five, 20 round UP launcher's. UP stood for Unrotated Projectile, which were 7in. diameter rocket propelled anti-aircraft weapons.*

Above, HMS Hood *in Scapa Flow, October 1940. The two images below are the last photographs taken of the* Hood, *from* HMS Prince of Wales, *while on their intercept course with the German battleship* Bismarck *and the heavy cruiser* Prinz Eugen, *the day before her loss. Both British warships are running at high speed.*

GENERAL STATISTICS

Dimensions (ft.)

length overall			860.60
beam			105.00
draught	as built	(min.)	28.50
		(max.)	31.50
	1931	(max.)	33.50
	1941	(max.)	33.85

Displacement (tons)

as built	light	41,200
	standard	42,700
	full load	45,200
1931	light	42,050
	standard	42,600
	full load	48,000
1939	light	42,750
	full load	48,650
1940	light	42,460
	full load	48,360

Propulsion

boilers	24	Yarrow small tube
engines	4	Brown-Curtiss Geared Turbines

propellers...4x manganese bronze 3 blade...diameter 15ft.

speed	1920	32.00kts
	1939	29.50kts
	1941	29.00kts
shaft horsepower	designed	144,000
	1920 trials	151,300
fuel capacity	1920	3,895 tons
	1931	4,615 tons
	1941	4,615 tons

Endurance

1920	7,500nm. @ 14kts
	5,000nm. @ 18kts
	4,500nm. @ 20kts
1931	8,900nm. @ 14kts
	5,925nm. @ 18kts
	5,332nm. @ 20kts

Armor (in.)

main belt	amidships	12, 7, & 5
	forward	6 & 5
	aft	6
	submerged	3
decks	forecastle	1.5
	forecastle amidships	2
	upper	1, .75, & 1
	main	1.5 & 2
	main over magazine	3
	lower deck forward	1.5 & 1
	lower deck aft	2 & 1
	steering gear	3
bulkheads		5 & 4
torpedo bulkheads		1.5 & .75
barbettes	A turret	12, 10, 6, & 5
	B turret	12, 6, & 5
	X turret	12 & 6
	Y turret	12, 9, 6, 5 & 2
conning tower		11 & 9; base 6 & 3; crown 5
director tower		6 & 3
after torpedo control tower		4 & 3
funnel uptakes		1.25
main turrets		15 face, 5 roof, 12 sides, 11 rear
secondary gun shields		1

anti-torpedo protection bulge built into hull.

Aircraft

1920-28	Fairey Flycatcher (2)
1931	Fairey 3F (1)

Complement

1920	78 officers	1,091 men
1931	98 officers	1,379 men
1941	94 officers	1,324 men

Cost

1920	Cost to build	£6,025,000.00
	Cost to maintain(year)	£274,000.00
1934	Cost to maintain(year)	£427,270.00

Armament

main	8x15in./42cal. in four twin turrets(1920-41)
secondary	12x5.5in./50cal. single mounts(1920-39)
	10x(1939-40) all removed 1940
torpedoes	x2 submerged(1920-37)
	x2 above water(1920-41)

AA armament;

4in. single mounts	x4(1920-37)
	x6(1937)
	x8(1938)
	x6(1939)
4in. twin mounts	x4(1939)
	x7(1940-41)
UP mounts	x5(1940-41)
2pdr. 8-barrel mounts	x2(1931-37)
	x3(1937-41)
0.50cal. quad mounts	x2(1933-37)
	x4(1937-41)

Ammunition

15in.	1920-'29	290HE, 672AP, 30 shrapnel & 82 practice.
	1929-'41	160HE, 640AP, 48 shrapnel & 96 practice.
5.5in.	1920-'29	1728 lyddite, 582HE, 96 shrapnel & 464 practice.
	1929-'40	1368HE, 624 shellite, 360HENT, 50 starshell & 450 practice.
4in.	1920-'39	600HE & 200 starshell.
	1939-'40	2000HE & 250 starshell.
	1941	4600.
40mm	1931-'37	11,520.
	1937-'41	17,280.
0.50cal.	1933-'37	20,000.
	1937-'41	40,000.

REFERENCES

Anatomy of the Ship - The Battlecruiser Hood
J. Roberts, Conway Maritime Press Ltd., 1982
The Bismarck Chase - New Light on a Famous Engagement
R. J. Winklareth, Chatham Publishing, 1998
British Battleships of World War Two
A. Raven & J. Roberts, Conway Maritime Press, 1976
Hood and Bismarck
D. Mearns & R. White, Channel 4 Books, 2001
Man O' War #6 - HMS Hood
M. Northcott, Bivouac Books Ltd., 1975
Naval Radar
N. Friedman, Conway Maritime Press, 1988
Naval Weapons of WWII
J. Campbell, Conway Maritime Press, 1985
Warship International #2/1972 - HMS Hood
D. G. Weldon, Naval Records Club, Inc., 1972
Warship Profile #19 - HMS Hood
R. G. Robertson, Profile Publications Ltd., 1972

RESOURCES

HMS Hood Association Web Site
www.hmshood.com

KM Bismarck Web Site
www.bismarck-class.dk

Thomas Schmid
thoschmid2@t-online.de

U. S. Naval Historical Center
Bldg. 57 Washington Navy Yard, Washington DC, 20374-2571
(202) 433-2765 www.history.navy.mil

U. S. National Archives
8601 Adelphi Rd. College Park, MD. 20740-6001
(301) 713-6800 www.nara.gov

This photograph from Warship Pictorial #19 shows the German battleship Bismarck *in the Baltic Sea, taken from the heavy cruiser* Prinz Eugen*, also the subject of Warship Pictorial #21.*

ACKNOWLEDGMENTS

Classic Warships
would like to express its gratitude
to the following individuals

Frank W. Allen, II &
HMS Hood Association Web Site
A. D. Baker, III

WARSHIP PICTORIAL SERIES

at the time of this printing

W. P. # 1 USS Indianapolis CA-35 - - - - *Out of Print*
W. P. # 2 USS Minneapolis CA-36 - - - - *Out of Print*
W. P. # 3 USS Louisville CA-28
W. P. # 4 USS Texas BB-35
W. P. # 5 USS San Francisco CA-38 - - - *Out of Print*
W. P. # 6 Omaha Class Cruisers
W. P. # 7 New Orleans Class Cruisers
W. P. # 8 USS Salem CA-139
W. P. # 9 Yorktown Class Carriers
W. P. #10 Indianapolis & Portland
W. P. #11 Lexington Class Carriers
W. P. #12 Benson/Gleaves Class Destroyers
W. P. #13 IJN Kongo Class Battleships
W. P. #14 USS Wichita CA-45
W. P. #15 KM Schnellboote - - - - - - - - *Out of Print*
W. P. #16 USS New Jersey
W. P. #17 IJN Myoko Class Cruisers
W. P. #18 USS New Mexico BB-40
W. P. #19 KM Bismarck
W. P. #20 HMS Hood
W. P. #21 KM Prinz Eugen

Upcoming titles:
W. P. #22 USS Ticonderoga CV/CVA/CVS-14
W. P. #23 Italian Heavy Cruisers of WWII

Cover Images: *The front cover is a collage by the author of one of Thomas Schmid's graphics and a real photograph of the ocean. The back cover is entirely a computer graphic presentation by Thomas Schmid.*